Vignettes

Vignettes

BETWEEN

TEARS

AND

LAUGHTER

by

ROSE CHORON

Illustrations by Rose Choron

Joseph Simon / **Pangloss Press**

1996

Library of Congress Catalog Card Number 96-69875

ACKNOWLEDGMENTS

These poems have appeared in the following publications:

Gradiva, Stony Brook University, New York: "Avatar" and "The Call of Muses." *Pearl,* Long Beach, California, and shortly in *The Pennywhistle Press,* New Mexico: "Sugar and Spice." *Pangloss Press,* Malibu California: "My Flesh And Blood." *Tucumcari Literary Review,* New Mexico: "The Zipper."

Published by Pangloss Press
P.O. BOX 4071, MALIBU, CALIFORNIA 90264
ISBN 0-934710-34-1

CONTENTS

I: REMINISCING

II: NEW YORK SKETCHES

III: OF ART AND MUSIC

IV: DREAMS AND VISIONS

In memory of Chaim Raphael, my dear Rab, a man of many wonderful colors and great zest for life, with whom I shared tears, laughter, and a beautiful friendship.

ROSE CHORON

I

REMINISCING

THE EAGLE

There were, as yet, no ski lifts,
no refreshments served on top of Alpine peaks.
We climbed the unspoilt mountains in the morning,
and came down on our skis for lunch.

On the last afternoon I felt quite sad,
anxious to scale the heights once more before I left.
"No one goes up there at this hour," I was told.
"Night falls abruptly, rather early, in these parts."
But I knew better.

I reached the summit by myself, and stood in awe,
a grain in the vast glacial desert,
all stillness and infinity.
There was no sign of life at this late time of day,
no bird, no tree, no human soul in sight.
The sun was just about to set, pink, frozen,
behind snow peaks rising from the fog below
like icebergs from the sea.

To dare the stately silence,
I broke into a yodel,
listening to echoes coming from all sides,
each peak responding separately, bidding me farewell.
Oddly, I sensed no fear in this stark whiteness.
Lulled by a youthful feeling of omnipotence,
I was convinced that no harm could occur to me
as long as I had *me* to look after myself.

Skis secured, I started down
the long, familiar trail.
The world was mine.
I was an eagle soaring through the air.

Dusk fell just as I reached the forest
steeped in fog.
A whiff of panic hit me.
I stopped to take a breath.
Tightening wits and muscles, I began creeping
between tree trunks in the dark,
eyes fixed intently on the ground,
groping my way along the icy track,
—a snail testing its feelers—
with but one thought: I'll make it!

Then suddenly, after what seemed a lifetime,
there was a clearing, and the fog had lifted.
The village, flooded by the moon, glowed reassuring in the distance.

I felt tears running down my cheeks,
and stood still, listening to the sounds around me:
church bells, a passing train, crows cawing.

A shaggy collie had come from a nearby farm
to look me over guardedly.
Responding to my strokes,
he bid me welcome with a friendly bark,
jumped up and licked away my tears.

FRANKA

Franka came running to alert her husband:
"Germans are on their way, looking for Jews!"
Ptachek just managed to shove his Jewish protégés
into the hole he had dug up for them
in the back of his barn.
"Go quickly, milk the cow outside," he pushed his wife.
"Try to distract the Huns when they arrive."
He, himself, grabbed a pair of shears,
and began pruning bushes,
whistling away as if he had no worry in the world.

When the three Germans came to this idyllic set up,
Franka greeted them with a sweet *"Grüss Gott."*
Her heart sank when she saw one entering the barn.
The others stopped and grinned at her.
She forced herself to smile, and poured milk
from her pail into their open palms.
They laughed and lapped it noisily,
calling out to their pal: "Come on Horst, have some fun.
To hell with the Jews!"
But Horst was devoted to his sacred cause.
"Gdzie sa paskudny Zydzi?" he yelled,
proud of the only sentence he had learned in Polish:
"Where are the dirty Jews?"
Ptachek spat on the grass and crossed himself.
"There are none here," he yelled back
with feigned indignation.

"Those damned Jews!" he thought to himself.
Why did he get involved with them?
It all was Franka's fault.
When Dr. Golden came to ask for shelter,
she had insisted that he hide him in their barn.
"He saved our son's life
when all other doctors failed," she said.
Besides, who knows, we might need him again."
Then, two weeks later, Ethel Weiss appeared with her two daughters, Ruth and Lea.
They too were frantic, looking for a refuge,
after the Nazis had shot Mr. Weiss.

Franka was adamant when Ptachek balked.
"I know these people like my family," she cried.
"I worked for them since I was fourteen.
They taught me cleanliness, the Bible,
how to read and write.
They made a better Christian out of me.
And don't forget! That's where we met
when you delivered milk and eggs to them.
You even did so, secretly, after Hitler invaded Poland.
You were a good man then. Don't disappoint me now!"

Ptachek was raging like a lion.
"You know what they did to our Jesus!"
"Our Jesus was a Jew himself," she screamed.
"Besides, whatever has been done to Him,
happened two thousand years ago.
You can be sure Mrs. Weiss was not present.
I only know she has been good to me,
and if you let them go, I'll go with them."

That's when he finally gave in.
But under one condition only:
In exchange for his shelter,
Ethel was to transfer to him
their house and factory after the war.
He reckoned that he would not have to wait too long,
considering Hitler's fiascos
in North Africa and Stalingrad.

As soon as Ethel yielded to his terms,
Ptachek went out and worked all night,
to make the refuge he had dug for Dr. Golden
big enough for the four of them.
That's where they'd all been hiding
for the last nine months.
They slept by day, not to be heard outside,
and were awake at night.
Then Franka let them out for a short while,
to eat, breathe, wash, relieve themselves,
and stretch their legs;
needs they had to hold back until she came.

This Sunday morning, though,
the radio had announced Russian soldiers
on the verge of liberating Poland.
Bursting with joy, Ptachek came to the barn,
carrying cake and wine to celebrate.

Just then, the Germans caught him by surprise.
Dirty, dishevelled, knowing, no doubt,
their days were numbered, they had come
to perform their last "heroic" deed.
If they were to discover the four Jews,
they'd kill them on the spot,
together with himself and Franka.

Ptachek dropped his shears.
He could not stand it any longer, and went into the barn
to see what Horst was up to.
There he was, searching the hay with a pitchfork,
picking it up in front, and throwing it to the back.
Unwittingly, he heaped it all above the Jewish hide-out.

His pals had come to watch him.
"Stop it," they kept urging him,
"there are no Jews here, can't you see? Let's go!"
Just when he was about to reach what he was looking for,
Horst flung his fork into the corner and decamped.

When Franka came at night to feed her little lot,
she found them wild-eyed, disoriented,
Ethel dead in her daughters' arms.
The shock had been too great for her weak heart.
Ptachek buried her near the barn, insisting, all along,
that Lea, just turned eighteen,
honor her mother's deal with him.

That night, Franka remained in the barn with her flock.
Her heart went out to the two orphans,
lost sheep, shorn of all right to live in dignity.
She blushed at the mere thought
of her own warm, clean bed.
"At least they are together," she tried to tell herself,
"each struggling to survive for the sake of the other.
And Dr. Golden's reassuring presence
gives them solace and support."

She remembered the first night
the women spent together with him
in their common cell.
How shy they were, and how embarrassed
to share their privacy with a young stranger!
To him, however, their arrival was a spark from heaven,
come to light up his loneliness.
He sensed their inhibitions and,
from the very start,
remained discretely in his corner.
With time, they grew to know, to need,
to like and to respect each other.
Conventions lost their relevance.
Yet, quite instinctively, they kept
at least a semblance of decorum,
not to let go and fall apart.
The women, for example,
called their new friend: "Dr. Golden,"
and he, too, addressed Ethel by her family name.

"He is a gentleman, a *Mensch,*"
she kept telling her daughters.
"What would we do without him?"

As he had studied medicine in Paris,
he spoke French fluently.
Sometimes, during long, dreary nights,
he'd sing *chansons* to them
by Maurice Chevalier or Edith Piaff.
They told each other dreams and stories,
played word games, made up puzzles.
He even tried to teach them French,
poems by La Fontaine, proverbs, nursery rhymes.

With Ethel gone, he now was the sole pillar
they had to hold on to.

Three days after her burial,
Ptachek came to announce their liberation.
Huddled up in a corner,
the sisters were too weak and numb to realize what happened.
With Dr. Golden's prompting,
they finally crept out.

Having lived in the dark so long,
it took them weeks to adjust to daylight.
As soon as Lea had somewhat recovered,
she made arrangements with the help of Dr. Golden,
to join their uncle in Jerusalem.
Diamonds Ethel had covered up as buttons
sewed to the blouses they had worn throughout,
tided them over for the next two years,
and paid their trip to Palestine.
Before they left, however, Lea officially transferred
their house and factory to Ptachek.

For a long time, she tried to keep in touch with Franka,
sending her letters, snapshots, Jaffa oranges for Christmas,
receiving no reply.

Years later, when she returned
to take her mother's remains to be buried in Jerusalem,
she learned that Ptachek died shortly after the Bolsheviks
had confiscated his farm and acquired properties.
Franka, now, lived and worked on a *kolkhoz*.*
All gifts and letters Lea sent from Israel,
had therefore never reached their destination.

When the two women met,
they fell into each other's arms,
crying, laughing, not knowing where to start.
Too many memories defied words, comprehension.

Lea took out some snapshots.
"That's Ruth in uniform," she said,
"a soldier in the Israeli army.
And here's my husband."
"It's Dr. Golden," Franka cried.
"And these boys are your sons?"
Lea was holding Franka's hand.
"That's right," she smiled.
"The older one is Chaim, Hebrew for 'life,'
and little Frankel has been named
after our Good Samaritan
to whom we owe our lives."

*Collective farm of the USSR

GALINA

She swings her generous curves
and autumn colors in a hammock
under sycamores,
Galina, earth goddess of my youth!

Her auburn mane tucked in a bun,
round, rosy-cheeked and smiling,
one child in her strong arms,
the others hanging on,

she doles out sweet milk
from her breast,
singing a Russian lullaby
in her deep, amber voice

that rocks us
into dreams of plenty.

AND THE BROOK BABBLES ON

Fir tops below my window
rock me back to our shtetl,
its fragrant, moss-lined
pine woods teeming with
bilberries, birds, butterflies.
We used to picnic there,
splash in the cool brook.

The forest is still standing.
A silent witness
to the carnage
committed in its shadow
not so long ago.
Each tree a tombstone
to lives shovelled
under its green carpet.

Now, Lithuanian children
picnic on that carpet.
My shtetl is *Judenrein.*

THE CHOO-CHOO TRAIN

The beach was empty
on this misty day.
We were the only ones around.
"Rain or shine, kids must be aired!"
That was Anni's Teutonic rule.

"You are a big girl now," she said,
unpacking our toys and shovels.
"Next year you're starting school.
So, I will leave you
with your brother for a while,
and you shall be his nanny
till I'm back.
Stay put, do not go near the sea!
The waves are high.
They swallow little children
if they come too close.

Off she went, leaving us
to our castles in the sand.
We dug canals, built towers, fortresses.
A little crab arrived, and then departed.
I ran to catch it, but it was too fast.

When I returned, David had disappeared.
Anni, a fuming fury,
was waiting for me, red with rage.
"Where is your brother?" she screamed,
"You bad girl!
I told you to look after him!"
I cried and cried, sure that the waves
had swallowed David, and that it was my fault.

The search took hours.
Mother came. So did the police.
Then, by sheer chance,
a guest from our hotel passed by.
"You're looking for your little boy?" she said,
"I saw him at the window of the toy shop."

There he was, in a trance,
watching the choo-choo train
in action, on display.
We cried, laughed, cuddled our dear deserter.
Mother showered him with caresses
and, of course, a choo-choo train.

As we got home, tired and relieved,
I felt a little sad.
Not knowing why, I locked myself
into the broom closet,
and fell asleep.

When it was time for dinner,
no one could find me.
Again, there was an endless search,
until I woke up in the dark, screaming,
forgetting where I was, unable to get out.

By no means did discovery of my whereabouts
elicit the elation caused by David's reappearance.
Instead of hugs and choo-choo train,
I was given a spanking.

DEATH OF A CARDINAL

It was a summer night
at a smart garden party.
In my sweet-sixteen
cool, bare-backed dress,
I sat next to
an eminent man of the cloth,
my father's age.

He virtually undressed me
with his gaze,
and reaching for an apple,
presented it to me:
"Please, Mademoiselle, please
have this luscious fruit!"
When I declined, he eyed me wistfully.
"Too bad!" he grinned,
"Eve had to eat an apple
to become conscious of her nakedness."

"You lecherous snake," I thought,
smiling angelically back at him.
"Really?" I chirped, all holy innocence,
"And who, pray, tempted Eve?"

Years later, I learned
from the head lines,
he'd been nominated Cardinal.
"A man of wisdom, worldliness,
spirituality," they said,
"known for his charming wit and ways."

Time passed and, by coincidence,
I spotted a few lines in small print
on the back page of my newspaper.
He'd been found dead in a suburban brothel.
His bad heart had forsaken him.

CASE HISTORY

a true story

A little girl runs off and screams.
A man stands in the doorway,
His private parts in view.

In broken English, pale, bewildered,
He denies it all.
The little girl was dreaming.

But law demands to know:
Did he, or did he not, and if he did,
Is he a criminal or mentally disturbed?

A Polish house painter, just recently arrived,
Frail, in his early thirties,
He shakes and stammers, numb with fear.

At the psychiatric ward I am assigned to test him.
His sole response to Rorschach,
"A monster with huge tail,"
Produces prompt consensus: He cannot match
His father's hovering phallus,
And has to show that he too is a man.

But still, he won't admit his action,
And children cannot witness in a court.
Tied to a cot and held by three strong men,

Electric rods are fastened to his head.
A mini shock will cause a paroxysm.
Then he will lose control and tell the truth.

I want to scream, to slam the door behind me.
Instead, I stay to hold his hand.
He thinks they want to punish him,

And with closed eyes, awaits his execution.
The minute he awakes, they shoot the question:
"Did you expose yourself?"

"I do not understand," he whispers, passing out.
Six hours later he comes to.
For lack of adult witnesses, he is dismissed.

II

NEW YORK SKETCHES

Encounter

The young man on the bus, across from me,
was talking to a lady at his side.
He listened eagerly and smiled,
his empty eyes wide open, and turned upward.

"What a beautiful voice you have!"
I heard him whisper.
"You must be very young and pretty."

"Thank you," she laughed,
and shook his hand when getting up to leave.

He sat quite pensive for a while.
Then, with his sensitive long fingers,
he began reading in a Braille book,
chuckling, laughing aloud,
completely unaware of his surroundings.

Suddenly he jumped up.
"Have we passed seventy second street?"
"We're almost there," I reassured him.
"That's where I'm going too."

We both got off together,
and while we waited at the corner
for the light to turn,
I asked about the book he had been reading.
"That was Playboy," he explained.
"Most people think it's just a sexy magazine.
Actually, it features some of our best authors.
Today, for instance, there's a short story
by Philip Roth."

I wondered whether pictures too
could be produced in Braille,
and if it was not Marilyn's curves,
rather than Philip's wit,
that prompted my blind friend to chuckle.

While we were walking down Fifth Avenue,
he asked me if I saw the lady sitting next to him.
"I think I made her day," he said.
"I liked her, and I told her so.
She seemed so young and lively.
But when I touched her hand,
it was all wrinkled.
I hope my disappointment did not show."

Then, with an impish smile,
he turned around as if to look at me.
"And may I know how old you are?"

"I'll let you hold my hand," I laughed,
and helped him cross the street.

BAG LADY

The Madison side-walk café
Boasts a French accent.
One orders hamburger,
The waiter calls out:
"Une côtelette hachée!"

A female bundle wrapped in rags,
Combs garbage bins along the street,
Her goods and chattels roped in bags
Around her waist.
In front of the café,
She pulls a yoghurt carton
From the trash,
And guzzles up its dregs.

A seated customer jumps up,
Tends her his plate:
"Please, lady, have my steak!"
"Eat your own crap!" she croaks,
Spits on the pavement,
And decamps.

PAVAROTTI

On the graffiti garnished subway,
I sat next to a buxom matron,
floating garbs covering her corpulence,
a big sombrero, her silver locks.

She held a cage,
and pointed at a golden bird
with a black halo,
vocalizing at the top
of its bel canto scale.

"This is my Pavarotti," she informed me.
"What an unusual breed!" I wondered.
"A coloratura nightingale, the color of canaries."
"You're almost right." she smiled.
"It's a canary coached by nightingales.
There's a school for birds
we attend regularly.
They learn by imitating nightingales,
kept for that purpose."

Fascinated, a lady stood by, listening,
unaware of the boy behind her
trying to cut off her shoulder bag.
A tall black man grabbed the thief's wrist:
"You little bastard, drop that knife!"
The knife fell to the floor,
and while the man dragged the boy
off the train at the next stop,
the culprit hissed:
"It's you the bastard, licking their ass!"

It all happened so fast, that many did not notice.
Doors closed, the train took off, and little Pavarotti
picked up its performance unperturbed.

A TAXI RIDE

It rained as if the sluices of the sky had opened.
Soaked through my winter layers,
I stepped into the cab, heading for Carnegie Hall.
"Let's take the park. It's faster,"
I suggested to the driver.
"The park is closed to traffic after 7 p.m." he grinned.
"Reserved for joggers, lovers, muggers."

As we took off, he began lilting
tunes of my swinging days:
"Stormy Weather," "Singing In The Rain," "Blue Sky."
"How come you know this music?" I exclaimed
"It's not of your time."
He turned his bushy head with pony tail and earring.
"Nor are Mozart and Bach," he laughed.
"Harold Arlen, Nacio Brown, Irving Berlin,
are great American classics.
I often sing their songs at the Red Barn in Soho.
You can applaud me there on Fridays after midnight.
Here is my card," he added, "I'm Brian Bellini,
if ever you'd want a ride,
with built in tenor free of charge."

When I returned after the concert,
I could not find my purse to pay the taxi.
Before I had a chance to worry,
the door man handed it to me.
Bellini had delivered it, money, keys,
credit cards untouched.

"What a rare bird in this much maligned Babel!"
I thought to myself.
Next day, I sent him disks of the fox-trot era,
sung by Bobby Short,
"with thanks to my new friend,
best singer among cab drivers,
best cabby among singers."

CONEY ISLAND OUTING

Highways drop mobs
onto white-hot sand.
Loudspeakers
outroar waves,
kites soar overhead.

Along the shore
peacocks sport muscles,
nymphs contours.
Their offspring
scream, splash, scramble
in the sea.

Matrons rock
flabby flesh
to bygone blues,
munch marshmallows,
pay tribute to the sun.

At night, sweat-worn,
mosquito marred,
all swarm
through fumes, horns,
bottlenecks, back
to their air-cooled cubicles,
recovering —
for next Sunday's outing.

III

OF ART AND MUSIC

Summer

SUGAR AND SPICE

"Piss into it!" he says,
Scrutinizing my landscape:
Tulips, anemones, peach trees in bloom,
against a sapphire sky.

"But spring is beautiful," I mutter,
"What's wrong with that?"
He chuckles "Marilyn too was beautiful,
And even her sweat smelled.
This only made her more appealing."

Sucking the pipe through rusty,
Smoke-worn teeth, he shuts his eyes.

Half-heartedly I take the brush,
Paint dark clouds into my blue sky,
A laundry line between the blossoms,
With washed out jeans and khaki shirts.

"Bravo!" he shouts. "You've got my point."
Then he unwraps his lunch.
A reeking limburger and a ripe, juicy pear.
"To each his own Marilyn Monroe," he grins.

HANS HOFMANN'S CLASS

"Push and pull, zat is my motto,"
he said in his Bavarian English.
"A pisher is only alive
if ze fickers in it push and pull.
C'est la vie. Tension et détente."

As a young man, he'd studied art in Paris
next to Matisse, his idol,
at La Grande Chaumière,
and now he liked to throw
leftovers of his French into the classroom.

"How does one push and pull
the figures in a picture?" we inquired.

"Viz contrasts, of course!
Light against dark, cool against warm,
shapes against spaces.
It's a continuous interplay
between colors, textures, forms.
Ze surface must never be static.
Push and pull gives us ze illusion
of movement."

Contrary to the linear perspective
of Renaissance masters,
Hofmann tried to create
depth on a flat surface,
by contrasts and juxtapositions,
and by shifting shapes
up and down, left and right.
His basic shapes were cubes, spheres,
cones, pyramids. He rarely used lines.

He now placed a painting on the easel,
and next to it a basket filled with
colored paper shreds and thumb tacks.

"Vot's wrong viz zis pisher?" he asked.
"It's falling apart," a student volunteered.
"Correct! It has no focus and no dynamo."

He tacked a speck of Prussian blue
onto the canvas, left of center.
"Zat pulls it in, *nicht wahr?*
But now it's dead."

"A red spot on the lower right
might resurrect it," a girl suggested.
"Vy not? Let's try!"
"Ah!" we exclaimed, that does it."
"Well, not quite," he mused. "Vy?"
"The red draws the eye out of the picture."
"*Richtig!* And how do we pull it in again?"
"Maybe with a bright violet cube
under the Prussian blue?"
"Bravo!" he shouted.
"Ze violet pulls ze red and blue togezer,
and gives ze pisher depth and gist.

Now you've got it:
Vee pulled ze pisher in viz blue,
pushed it out viz red,
and drew it togezer viz violet, *nicht wahr?*
Zat's how you push and pull
ze fickers in a pisher."

SEASONS PUT TO MUSIC

In vibrant autumn hues,
passionate and celestial,
the cello's female curves
send forth a desperate lovesong
of the dying swan
immortalized by Saint-Saëns.

Winter evokes a fugue by Bach,
bold, unadorned, transparent,
a cool brook with warm undercurrents,
played on a harpsichord.

Debussy's sparkling raindrops
ring across the keyboard,
clear like crystal beads,
spell spring showers,
impressions by Seurat.

Summer is a symphony,
a pastorale à la Vivaldi.
Turtledoves coo, larks warble,
lambs bleat to shepherds' pipes,
woodpeckers tap the rhythm.
A sudden flash of lightening
strikes from the blue.
Thunderbolts blast the air.
The sky dims, drums drone, trumpets blare,
till tender violins, flutes,
appease the storm *cantando con amore.*

MERRY-GO-ROUND

Shrinks thrive on airing
constipated psyches,
often relieved on canvas
as fine art.

Proud connoisseurs,
why, even shrinks,
pay pretty pennies
for such primal products.

That's what propels
the carousel.

IV

DREAMS AND VISIONS

PISCES

I am a trout
caught in a tank,

longing to be
at large,

to ride wild currents,
jump cascades,

catch minnows,
flicker fins,

have sun-rays
dancing on my scales,

and oh, be free
to bite or

not to bite
a bait.

FIREWORKS

The limousine taking me uphill
to my promised man,
unfurls into a hearse.
His Plymouth ancestors,
embedded in clear ice blocks,
stare at me, eyes agape.

The car starts rolling backwards,
gains speed, crashes
against his Steinway
standing at the bottom of the road.
Keys, strings, lid, sounding board
burst into fireworks
propelled across the blazing sky.

At the wheel of my Land-Rover,
I take off soaring
through the poppy speckled
spring of Galilee,
singing the *Hatikvah.*

magna mater

with love-trimmed baits
the sea tugs
the young dolphin

to her womb.
he tumbles in her tides
wallows in her luxuriance.

beware oh innocent
lest you be prey
she feeds to feed on!

CERES

I'm put to sleep for my Caesarian,
sent off to sunflower lit prairies.

Ceres, in a white tunic,
wheat sheaves around her flaming mane,
offers gifts from a horn of plenty,
sweet grains of corn, bran, rye,
to ducklings just out of shells,
piglets at mother's teats.

Clouds gather, burst into tears.
Ceres stands drenched,
a blown out torch,
her eyes cast down on
what I dare not see . . .

desert

spinoza spins
red spider webs

across sahara's
snow-capped peaks

where pussy-willows
play with tiger-lilies

frogs waltz
to fog horns

and we devour
each-other's halo

napoleon's hat

head-shaven, naked and erect,
i sit under arcades,
archaic and deserted.
far off, i see red stains.
i rise and say:
"this is blood of my womb."
a voice protests:
"no, no, these are anemones."
indignant, i put on
napoleon's hat.
"this is my blood," i shout,
and walk into the sea.

my flesh and blood

a cow is in my room.
she stands in a far corner
quiet undemanding
as if apologizing
for the imposition.
I realize that I forgot
to feed her.
she must be hungry.

but my bin is bare.
two meager veal chops
and a mug of milk.
she gulps it all
and looks at me
with grateful trusting eyes.
I know the food is wrong
in quantity and kind.

she swallows
her own flesh and blood.
but can I give more than I have?
she should be on a farm
get proper care
while I would come to visit.
yet I can't part with her.
I love her.

she is my flesh and blood
so good and true
giving forgiving
oh so wise.
I put my arms around her
feel her warmth
and waking to bright cow-bells
turn off the alarm.

V

PAINTED POEMS

Bella Vista

Into my window-frame
grows an Abruzzi village,
crumbling and archaic.

It rises from the rock,
vine-clad, poppy-freckled.
Grey olive trees
lift crippled limbs
in homage to some god.

I walk its tortuous lanes.
Dandelions peep
through cracks of cobblestones,
old folks gossip
on benches in the sun,
cats play mating games,
children jump rope.

A fragrant field of lavender
veils breezes
from the public *pisciatoio.*

NOSTALGIA

Trees yawn with outstretched arms,
waving farewell to summer,
tucked away in leaf quilts
for its yearly nap.

Perched on a pole,
a lone grouse drowses,
one eye on the watch
for some marauding Nimrod.

Seasonal workers shear sheep,
hum hymns in minor keys
to hovels left in Burgos, Andalusia,
remembered from afar
as heavenly haciendas.

TO GRANDMA MOSES

Kids slide on silent sleds
Over whipped wedding cakes
Their bright-hued parkas
Rainbows against cerulian skies

Drab townships wrapped in white
Turn into hamlets snug unruffled
Smiling at the moon
Pretending to protect them

paradise enow

a loaf of bread
wine cheese and
red cheeked peaches

clusters of grapes
white lilacs
in a vase

their fragrance
filling
my whole being

the table is set
for two
awaiting you

bomb-site

daffodil-decked debris
ghosts of former glory
drowse under unblemished skies

I blush at seeing beauty
in these ashes
of atrocities

reach for my palette
frame the folly
of it all

PRIMAVERA

Spring spreads a wedding train
of blossom-dotted orchards.

Sunshowers paint rainbows,
spray confetti,
larks serenade, the air gets drunk
on lilacs, jasmine, peonies.

A liberated, pregnant bride,
the earth, in constant labour,
keeps heaving sprouts into the light,
to celebrate her reawakening.

Primavera

VI

MUSINGS

Mirror

You are the truest friend,
dependable, unbiased,
reflecting us just as we are.

Some, you alert:
"Go see the doctor!
You look sick."

Others you reassure:
"Don't mind your weight!
You are a beautiful Maillol."

It takes great courage, though,
to face you when your verdict
is unpleasant, irrevocable.

I love you when you show me off,
but apprehend
your biting frankness.

Just tell me if my hair
needs combing, if colors clash,
or if my dress is torn!

spell

spellbound
I spelled out
what I felt

gave birth
with triumph
to the word

now that
I spelled it out
I mourn the

spell

the call of muses

I fight
my cumbrous years
mourn somersaults
untethered spirit
would to forget
the unretrievable
yield but to insights
and the call of muses

the beautiful people

hair tousled, togged in minks
over frayed jeans, soiled sneakers,

she doles out smiles and coins,
like morsels to her poodle,

to him who opens doors,
hails cabs, bows deeply,
hides his grin.

nirvana

to float
on nothingness
in primal stillness!

oh but to be
and not
to have to!

Who holds the key to the big door?

Who guards the secrets that explain
whatever there has been before?
Who pulled the trigger, who's to blame
for Black Holes and for Big Bang's roar?

We know the cause of sunshine, rain,
we conquer space, invent, explain
all things except: what was before
the Black Hole and the Big Bang's roar?

Whence did the spark come, whence the core?
Who planned it all? Which master brain
composed the code, touched off the chain?
There must have been something before!

Who holds the key to the big door?

The Creation

WALTZING ON

Hats off to the Methuselah
Who thumbs his nose
At creaky knees,
Embraces Schubert, Mozart, Bach,
Holds hands with Shakespeare's
Beautiful Dark Lady,
Waltzing on towards the beyond!

VII

HERE AND BEYOND

avatar

the earth
has sucked you

into her
worm-worn womb

and from it fresh
forget-me-nots

reach for
the sun

spectral visions

I tend poor oldsters
relics of themselves
bereft of memory mobility

shudder at spectral visions
of my own self
years from now

tense wits limbs muscles
to keep fit
and to dodge hell on earth

on the dim way to heaven

COPING

I'm living on.
I eat, I sleep,

I laugh,
make love,

enjoy the spring,
Picasso, Bach.

Am I betraying you
who are no more?

I close my eyes
and see yours

caring, wise.
You dwell with me

in dreams
and in my heart.

To carry on without,
I carry you within.

WHY?

Had you but whispered
your despair, asked us for help!

You shunned our love,
yielded to lodestones
that have lured you under,
took to the grave a whole world
which was yours to be.

Faced with the irrevocable,
shattered by guilt
for some vague,
uncommitted crime,
we try to contain
pain, compassion, anger
and to accept
your final deed.

Nostalgia

VIII

HAPPY ENDINGS

THE ZIPPER
(a pantoum)

Who needs a bombshell like Monroe
After a sumptuous Sunday meal!
Deliberating where to go,
He yields to Marilyn's bust appeal.

After a sumptuous Sunday meal,
Relaxed, he eases belt and zipper.
He yields to Marilyn's bust appeal,
Enjoys the film, and feels quite chipper.

Relaxed, he eases belt and zipper.
A lady comes. He lets her by,
Enjoys the film, and feels quite chipper.
Rising for her, he zips his fly.

A lady comes. He lets her by,
When suddenly he feels a pull.
Rising for her, he zips his fly,
While the crowd howls: "Sit down, big bull!"

When suddenly he feels a pull,
He knows his zip has caught her dress.
While the crowd howls: "Sit down, big bull!"
He thinks: "Hell, now I'm in a mess!"

He knows his zip has caught her dress.
The usher flashes a big light.
He thinks: "Hell, now I'm in a mess,
There's no way out, nowhere to hide."

The usher flashes a big light.
People scream: "Sit down! We can't see!"
There's no way out, nowhere to hide.
Oh, what a tragicomedy!

People scream: "Sit down! We can't see!"
The lady whispers: "Let's get out!
Oh, what a tragicomedy!"
both push their way through in a bout.

The lady whispers: "Let's get out!"
They are attached like Siamese twins.
Both push their way through in a bout.
The scene is set. Romance begins.

They are attached like Siamese twins.
He asks forgiveness, in distress.
The scene is set. Romance begins.
She laughs, though he has ripped her dress.

He asks forgiveness, in distress.
Enamoured, they leave hand in hand.
She laughs. Though he has ripped her dress,
Their fiasco has a happy end.

Enamoured, they leave hand in hand,
Deliberating where to go.
Their fiasco has a happy end.
Who needs a bombshell like Monroe!

a roast by any other name

manhattan clam chowder
tastes better à la française
as "bouillabaisse"
and good old boston beans
as "cassoulet" in nîmes

in china town one can't go wrong
with kreplakh soupe
they call "won ton"

custard proffered as "crème brulée"
hamburgers as "côtelettes hachées"
will flatter palates any day
as will beef stroganoff ragout
in fact each but a dressed up stew

yet no dish needs to yield its name
if graced with gold-rimmed chilled champagne

People And Their Pets

Some are too shy
To show affection
For fear of
Facing a rejection
They pour it all
Upon their cat
Who loves them
Even dumb and fat

To others
Somewhat domineering
Their dog
So servile and endearing
Provides obedience
Hard to get
From anyone
Except a pet

But for
The very young and old
Animals are
To hug and hold
To talk to
Caress love and feed
Or tease a bit
To serve their need

laughs best who laughs last

women past seventy
pass as passées

men in their seventies
as charming roués

regardless of feminists'
great liberation

nothing will change
this sad situation

yet while women past eighty
may still hop around

their charming roués
often rot under ground

MY GALLERY

My Gallery

Cézanne

You aged like Burgundy, Cézanne,
Mellowed through years, surpassed by none,
And with Mont Sainte Victoire's ascent,
You reached your summit in the end.

Chagall

Chagall, I love your early dreams.
The later ones, to me it seems,
Are often stereotyped, regressing,
A Russian salad with French dressing.

Degas

Degas portrayed, with great devotion,
His ballerinas caught in motion,
Thoroughbred horses, lean and fast,
Snapshotlike oils, pastels and casts.

Braque

Georges Braque, the Bach of cubist art,
(His Fauve creations set apart,)
Composed bold fugues, calm and serene,
Where all sides of each thing are seen.

Picasso

Picasso's blue, pink, cubist pearls,
His one-eyed, two-nosed pin-up girls,
Uprooted former generations,
Opened wide doors for new creations.

Bonnard

Interiors sunny, orange, pink,
A woman sponging at the sink,
Views from a bay-window ajar,
Casual meals: that's Pierre Bonnard.

Matisse

Matisse, the lion of the Fauves,
Green nudes, red fields, blue trees, pink groves,
Turned handicap into an asset,
With cut-outs as his final facet.

Monet

Monet caught gardens, nénuphares,
Haze-bathed cathedrals, smoke filled "gares,"
Elegant picnics, stacks of hay,
At various hours of the day.

Van Gogh

Van Gogh pours out his passion, lust,
his love, unfulfilled yearnings,
Imparts to us his plight and pain
Through brush strokes wild and burning.

Renoir

Renoir's poppy fields, country fairs,
Rosy-cheeked children, dancing pairs,
Beautiful maidens, buxom, lush,
Spell joie de vivre with sensuous brush.

Gauguin

Gauguin, though quite a ruthless man,
Caught magic moods of Pont-Aven,
And of Tahiti's earthy queens
Set in exotic, dreamlike scenes.

Pissaro

Pissaro's peaceful hamlets, farms,
His blooming orchards, "grands boulevards,"
Reflect the essence of all France,
its "savoir vivre" and "élégance."

Kandinsky

Kandinsky the experimentor,
Cerebral artist and inventor,
the Bauhaus genius of precision,
Possessed great discipline and vision.

Klee

Our brilliant dreamer, dear Paul Klee,
On sparing space has much to say.
A whimsical, creative mind,
Great master of the playful kind.

Fauves

Dufy, Derain, Marquet and Braque,
One day broke out as a wild pack.
After three years of gentle rage,
They all returned to their old cage.

Jackson Pollock

He runs around huge sheets and doodles,
Dripping from cans bright, entwined noodles.
That's Jackson Pollock caught in action.
The result is a great attraction.

Minimalists

Patrons and connoisseurs behold
A heavy board, white, sleek and bold,
As essence of all things untold,
For which they pay its weight in gold.

Anal Expressionists

Baselitz's reversed fecal smears
Equal Gober's urine veneers.
Like tots, proud of each burp and fart,
Such daubers call their products art.

ROSE CHORON: psychologist, painter, writer, divides her time between New York and Switzerland. Aside from various poems that appeared in British and U.S. magazines, she wrote a narrative poetry book, "Family Stories," and translated Daniel Stauben's 19th Century French memoirs, "Scenes of Jewish Life in Alsace," both published by Pangloss Press, Malibu, California.